Good Mourning Hopeful Night

Francis Spillane

ISBN-10: 197-4099520
EAN-13: 978-1974099528

This book is dedicated to my mother, Cynthia D. Rohde, who taught and encouraged me to write and to live, always with honesty and from the heart.

"You've gone, but we are still with you.

We remain, and you are still here;

forever together and forever family—

bound in love eternally."

CONTENTS

V.

PREFACE

This collection of poems began in an outpouring of grief during a time of immense loss, and quickly became a means of healing from that loss. As I continued to write, I discovered that they were also a method of finding new purpose and direction, and that writing these poems helped to foment a new urgency, and a new seriousness and thankfulness towards my relationships with others, and with God.

As I shared these poems with others I saw how they touched on familiar emotions and experiences, and elicited interesting, and in some cases deeply meaningful responses and disclosures. It then occurred to me that by baring my grief to others through these poems, sharing my journey of healing, and the discovery of my deepening relationship with God, that it might help, inspire and encourage others on their own paths.

I want to acknowledge and thank all of the family and friends who have encouraged me in my writing and who also gave helpful feedback along the way. I specifically want to thank Sonia Barry, who's painting, *The Poppies,* appears in this book, Father John Strickland for being a vocal advocate for my writing, and Dr. Gregg Jantz for his encouragement to publish. Photos were obtained from pxhere.com and are in the public domain.

When the time comes for sorrow and grief — as it does for each of us — my hope is that we all may find our way to a "good mourning". When we find ourselves in the depth of darkness, in a night that seems never to end, that we not despair; but pray and wait — and hopefully shed tears that wash our souls, relieve our distress, and help us see clearly that the night is full of hope; and the potential for a joyful morning is not far off.

~Francis Spillane

Cynthia D. Rhode
Poppies
Weaving

INTRODUCTION

I would like to provide a little context, to set the stage for the poetry that follows, by sharing a little of my own personal history:

None of us knew what we had, until it was gone — or if we did know, in part — we didn't fully understand; until it all became just a memory.

In his prime, my step-father had a regal bearing; he was tall, and stood even taller in my thoughts and feelings towards him. He wore turtlenecks, which to me as a child, added to his stature and somehow gave his face and frame a look of royalty.

I also admired my father — more for his mind and helpful advice, than for what he wore. Also, he was kind; and aside from a certain disquiet in his soul, which led to a recurring dalliance in some life choices, he was otherwise trustworthy and a man of integrity.

My mother was all things to me and though we had our disagreements, we also had each other's backs, and we faced the world's assaults together.

My brother was eleven years older than me, and so, we didn't know each other very well. We were amicable but generally distant; this, in part, due to the difference in age, but more due to his reclusive nature. Over the years I came to accept this distance and that he preferred to live as a bit of a hermit — at least towards his family — and that we probably would never really be very close.

So I was surprised when he invited me one day to have lunch with him and spend the afternoon in the redwoods. He even went to the trouble of making cheese sandwiches for us and packing them, along with sodas, into brown lunch bags for our outing. After thirty-eight years we finally had lunch together; and we became friends. This led to semi-regular phone calls to each other and discussions about sports cars, foreign and domestic, and other important life matters.

We enjoyed one more lunch together, about two years later. This time he treated my wife and me to a meal at his favorite Japanese restaurant — the kind where they cook the meal there at your table. There was an exquisite intimacy in that meal: the gift of his time, the quietness and the laughter shared between the three of us, the warmth and the affection, the glasses of red wine.

I will always remember the red wine, so pretty in the glass. My brother loved red wine. Sometimes he loved it too much. A month after this meal, on his way home from a dinner with a friend, he was pulled over and arrested for driving while intoxicated. Because of this he lost his license, and then his job as a bus driver, and a few weeks later he shot himself.

Our last phone conversation, a few days earlier had focused on God, death and the afterlife. I suppose he was mulling his options — though I only understood that — too late.

Several months later my step-father fell and broke his hip. He went to a rehab center but his health slowly began to decline. We hoped for a recovery; however, week by week he lost strength. One day while my mom and I were visiting him he asked me to give his face a shave. He had an electric razor on the nightstand beside his bed.

Here it was again, that exquisite intimacy: the gift of his time, the quietness, the warmth and affection, just as it had been during that last meal with my brother. Here I was shaving the face of that man I always admired, that royal face. I did the best with my moment, and the honor I was given in caring for him in this way; I'm sure it wasn't the best shave he'd ever had but that wasn't for lack of trying on my part.

There is something else to say about my step-father because it is so beautiful and so endearing; he loved life with a childlike enthusiasm. There are many numerous examples from his life of this fact, but what remains with me now is from our final minutes together, the last ones I would spend with him alive. On this last visit, just before I left, he asked me to push him in his wheelchair around the corridors of the rehab center.

The main hallway outside his room made one large circle, and lining the walls were paintings and large photographs. As I pushed him around this circuit he asked me to stop at most of these, and we admired them together. They were of trees, or landscapes mostly, while some were of sunsets or sunrises. Of each he had multiple comments as to their beauty and how much they meant to him, or how they reminded him of his childhood, or some other time in his life. Each painting or photo was greeted with appreciation; and he approached each one, in the same way he lived each day, it seems, with gratefulness and benevolence — just as one would expect of a royal and noble man such as he.

As my mom explained it to me over the phone, she was with him several weeks later, holding his hand as he was sleeping. While he peacefully slept, he graciously stepped into the next world, breathing one moment — and not the next.

Years later my mom would explain that he was the true love of her life. In the manner and tone with which she explained this however, she also conveyed the truth that she never really understood this fact at the time, or expressed it to him fully while they were together — and she wished she had.

I hadn't seen or spoken with my dad for several years. I had joined a spiritual community in my early twenties and had been living a nomadic life — traveling, living and working in various states — which precluded much contact with friends and family. To earn money I did landscaping work and sold this service door to door. One day I was out walking the streets, knocking on doors as I typically would do in the afternoon, when I felt certain I was about to see my dad.

It was one of those rare times in my life when I sensed that what was about to happen would be an important and seminal moment. As his car came up the street I stepped off the curb and flagged him down. In my childhood, he and I had been affectionate, he was not afraid to give me a hug, but I can't remember a time that we ever held each other's hands. I got into his car and we began to talk and to catch up on each other's lives. And as we spoke we took each other's hands. It was such an unnatural thing for us to do, and yet, it felt extremely natural.

Our time was short as he was late for an appointment and had to get going. I felt an urgency to tell him how much I loved him, and my gratitude for his role in my life. He expressed similar feelings of love and affection, and all the while we kept holding hands. I will always remember how unusual, how strange, and also how wonderful that was.

Later that year I called my mom and she had the difficult task of telling me that my father had died several months earlier. They had tried to find me, to tell me, so I could go to the funeral but they had no way to contact me; and didn't know where I was, or how to reach me. She was so sorry that I didn't know about his death but I explained to her that I did know. I knew back then in his car, as we were holding hands, that I would never see him again; and that this would be the last time to hold him, and to express my true feelings for him.

Not long ago my mother also stepped into the next world — having taken her last breath for the journey — and leaving my sisters and I with a house full of memories. Our final months together were filled with tenderness and intimacy. She could hardly say a word and she spent most of her days and nights with her eyes shut and seemingly asleep, but she knew when we were near.

As she lay in her bed, we held wordless conversations — communicating love through the simplicity of touch. She had beautiful silver hair, and while it had thinned considerably, she still enjoyed occasionally having it combed; and it was a joy to have the opportunity to do that for her.

My heart is filled by the memory of her thinning hair, her sunken cheeks and deep eye sockets, her bruised papery skin and bony hands; all things which sound ugly and disturbing, and yet to me, as I saw them on her, were symbols and representations of perfect beauty; because she could be nothing less than supremely beautiful to me in whatever appearance she presented.

Of course I have surrounded myself with photos of her in earlier times: smiling photos, full of life, joy and health. These also are beautiful, but the memories that now fill me most with love and gratitude are from these final months together — while death began to pull us apart — dwelling within that exquisite intimacy.

I.

Many Tears

The angel of death blew in from the west—
not raging or howling, with only a whisper.
Yet with it came turmoil, a horrible test—
and darkness so black I recoiled in terror.

She passed in the night, and when I awoke,
the vessel I sail in was far out to sea—
ripped from its moorings, its bow lines all broke,
my port a small glimmer and difficult to see.

Returning was fruitless, the winds were against me;
the sun and the moon and the tides all were too—
thrusting me further and further to sea,
my home port retreating, retreating from view.

Dense fog pressed me in, my way was obscured—
thoughts swirling within me, found no place to land.
Distinctions, discernments, all lines were now blurred—
my vessel adrift, occupied yet unmanned.

I fell to my knees calling out to the heavens,
"Help me, save me, oh Lord of my life—
remove this cruel fog, reveal your clear presence,
show me the way into daylight my Christ."

The fog didn't clear, my anxieties mounted;
I slumped in despair, my hoping in tatters—
trapped in an eddy, all my powers confounded,
I awaited my doom now, and certain disaster.

This darkest of nights seemed to wear on—
interminably, incessantly, time upon time.
No harbinger arriving to announce a new dawn—
only mist and haze, keeping me blind.

If only the psalmist were right when he wrote:
that joy, our true joy will come in the morning—
weeping shall only tarry for the night,
and sorrows, our sorrows shall all have an ending.

The memory of things that she loved made me sad:
flowers and colors and scripture and song—
my tears started flowing, for which I was glad,
as the murk began parting which had plagued me so long.

Tears led to tears for her and for me—
for loss of the goodness we shared through the years.
And sorrow for my own inadequacies—
which keep me from loving because of my fears.

With the tears that I shed, the fog fell away,
as scales from my eyes, revealing the day.

The night of my sorrows was finally ending,
the psalmist was right, it was a good mourning.

Crumpled Paper

Feeling like a crumpled piece of paper,
wet and muddy,
left in a corner of an empty house—
cracked windows, dusty floors,
someone puked on the tiles.

When I think of what is lost now,
nausea also rises in me—
delirium, vertigo and an overflowing melancholy;

with tears too wet for words.

While words are helpless to express
this thing which really can't be shared.

But there is hope;
I am told, and I believe it—
a sun and a light breeze which will blow
through these hollow inner rooms—

breathing new life,
straightening what is crumpled,
and healing what is sick.

True Home

Our mother created
a comfortable and peaceful place,
a true home in every sense of the word.

We were delivered
out of difficulties and lonely spaces,
into a warmth which radiated love.

Her home was always opened
to those who needed a kindly face,
and hers was most kind and full of light.

Now she is gone.
Her home will be sold;
and we are left to find our own way.

We search drawers and closets
hoping to be consoled,
finding solace in anything that speaks of her.

Sharing words
about her home and her life extolled,
huddling in the shadows left by a setting sun.

We are tempted to remain here,
looking towards our past,
turning this place into a museum.

But grace will not allow us,
sending plagues to disturb our rest,
forcing us to flee towards freedom.

Calling us to seek a better place,
enjoying an eternal feast,
meeting again in another house, with many mansions.

The Tremor

I felt a tremor today
in my heart.
I barely took notice
as I did my daily work.

I sensed a larger problem deep within,
a tremendous shaking on the other side of my soul,
foretelling a tsunami of sorrow rising.

I wish I could be someone else today,
writing something different—

something funny, and witty,
with a surprising and ironic twist at the end;
not soft and emotionally raw,
from the heart, and uncomfortable to read.

Spillanes are supposed to write crime novels,
not poems about feelings.
The main character is supposed to be tough and cool—
dames, with slender legs dangling off the corner of his desk;
not a man with a girl's name, writing about his broken heart—
treacly, sentimental and soft.

Life presents us with reality, and it isn't what it is supposed to be.

I don't get to be the detective with the fedora and raincoat.

Still, maybe I can uncover the missing emotion,
and help someone find a long lost love,
hidden within them—
by way of example.

A Standing Shell

When the inside has crumbled,
how can the outside still stand?
This question I ponder
as I survey the devastation within me,
left behind by the loss of my mother.

Strength, courage, comfort and joy,
wander aimlessly amidst the rubble.
Shell-shocked little children,
groping in the dark, searching for the light.
While anxiety plunders me, unabated.

It seems implausible that the whole edifice
hasn't come crashing down.
Flesh and blood, so solid and heavy,
suspended by what:
determination, will, fear?
Keep me standing lest I fall, never to get up again.
Faith, hope, love?
A cord of three strands not easily broken,
invisible and difficult to understand.

Time heals all wounds,
and time turns everything here to dust;
our lives are sung out to a constant refrain of goodbyes.

Now a chorus of sorrow,
but tomorrow voiced with a strain of sweetness,
and eventually, full-throated shouts of eternal joy.

The aimless will be reoriented,
and the dust will be reanimated.

What is now suspended around a fallen core,
Will be enlivened into life forevermore.

Not A Rhetorical Problem

How can we possibly hear
the quiet and still voice of God
and understand the promise of eternity
amidst the shrill cacophony of death?

My senses are tumbled and my mind reels
at the constant, steady drip—drip—drip—
of the loves I have lost—lost—lost.

While the hope of eternal reunion is an image
seen darkly, at best, through a clouded glass;
I see clearly the path and trajectory of this life,
slipping away,
and all I hold dear—
dying before my eyes.

Prayer binds the wounds and soothes the pain,
for a time,
but then—
the misery of death marches on.

I'm a child with little true understanding
and I cannot pretend to understand,
nor can I play games to distract me
from what I see or from what I feel;
snacks and funny movies don't help me forget.

What recourse do I have here
if I am honest with myself?

Just time, and the passage of time?

There may very well be a future hope
and a life eternal, I do believe it.

But flesh and emotion are howling now.

Perseverance and patience
through the suffering;
I can feel it—

Within the ashes of my loss
there remains an ember of love:

a small heat with potential to reignite.

I need God's breath to blow across me again—
to bring resurrection and renewed conflagration,
to bring a fire of love that enkindles my limbs,
and enlightens my life,

while I live.

Shedding

Death—
like a python,
slithers upon us.
All teeth;
piercing our flesh,
making us cry out
in anguish.

Then a long, slow
constriction:
suffocating
and
smothering.

Hope—
like a beacon,
shines upon us.
All glorious:
warming our flesh,
causing us to sing
for joy.

Then a peace
enfolding:
invigorating and
inspiring.

Teetering between
death and hope:
oscillating
and
careening.

Life—
like a promise,
of death postponed.

All dewy;
charming our senses,
helping us to forget
our end.

Then an unwelcome
intruding:
unraveling
and
awakening.

Christ—
like a thief,
takes everything.
All dreams;
removing our illusions,
leaving us with Him
alone.

Then a time of
suffering:
ennobling
and
deifying.

The Astounding Words of Job

The Lord gives and the Lord takes, blessed be the name of the Lord.
A better man than I spoke these words many years ago.
Although I must admit I love the way they roll off the tongue.

Blessed be the name of the Lord—
even though He allowed my life to be torn asunder.

Though He gave me my life,
He'll also allow it to be taken,
along with all the others.

How strange.

The armies of despair have camped round about me,
and are knocking at the door.
I've fought them off with prayer and with hope,
with tears and with sincerity,
with everything I've known to do,
and yet here they are again.

There are five stages of grief they say, I've read about them;
in fact, I read Kubler-Ross preemptively,
to get a jump on grief, and get a head start to healing,
so I could defeat despair and be whole.

But here they are—
the armies of despair knocking at my door,
threatening to tear me down.

The Lord gives and the Lord takes, blessed be the name of the Lord.
Can you imagine saying this and meaning it?

How strange and how beautiful.

Speaking of the stages of grief, I did them all;
and then I did them again,

and then I did them backwards,
and then I did the first one, skipped to the fourth,
backtracked to the second, and then the third,
and wrapped it up with the fifth.

And then I did that in reverse order just to be thorough.

But here we are—
despair and I looking at each other through the peephole.

Somebody has got to blink.

Am I just a toy on a string for the heavenly powers to play with?
Is it fun to watch me bleed,
and then to bind me up;
and then to bleed me yet again?

Job, how can you say it—
can you teach me how to say it too?

And to really mean it?

II.

Sonia Barry
Poppies, 2017
Acrylic on Canvas

Poppies

See the poppies grow
by the wayside.
Announcing summer's joy
against a passing snow.

Their glistening ruby
red infusing blooms,
do tame the stark and bitter
winds; each flower to obey.

As love's messengers
they dance before our eyes,
with warm vitality
and hope which long endures.

Hear them sing
of coming days so bright,
an end to frigid winter's night,
a balm to sooth the dreary.

See the poppies grow,
within their petals healing—

and marvel at their beauty
against the snow.

Imprinting

When I was born
I looked up into her eyes—
and I dwelt in love.

She held me
in her arms, and close
to her breast.

Her skin was cool,
my thoughts were warm—
at peace and in comfort.

Soothed by the maternal
hum and thrum
of her heart.

***

Through water,
the Lord led me in,
from my wandering.

He led me
into my heart—
where peace blossoms.

I see His beauty
and understand;

I am cradled in mercy.

My thoughts are stilled;
I can hear, and feel, and know—
the birthplace of Love.

Waiting

Perhaps there is no greater thing
than to wait.

Through waiting we are humbled.

Our lofty thoughts
are brought back to earth,
and we see that we are hungry—

like little birds
searching the sky for our mothers.

There is nothing to be done.
So we wait.

The world,
crashing and clambering around us,
tall trees cracking overhead,
in a violent wind.

We huddle down in our nests,
wondering what is next:

our hearts beating the time along—
breaking a little too.

We discover, the food that we sought from our mothers,
comes instead, through our own broken hearts:
glistening sap,
streaming forth honey—
amber love on fire,

feeding us from the hand of God.

Three Names

When you were born you were so small;
and you had blue eyes shaped like almonds.

Your mom thought you looked like her mother;
and your dad thought you looked tough.

That's why they named you Kirk, after Kirk Douglas.
But Kirk is also the church, the house of the spirit.
Your house had potential.

Twenty-three years later you left home,
seeking adventure and true life.
And you were named Francis.

Childhood ended.
Duty began.
Potential became kinetic.

But you still lived for yourself—
every movement to satisfy your belly,
and to win love from others.

Twenty three years later you died in water;
and your new life began.
And you were named John—
God is good.

The spirit dwells within his church now;
kinesis turning toward stillness and peace;
unfocused motion resolving into hesychasm.

Then your mother died—
and again you died,
not in spirit or in body,
but in some strange, intangible way—

shaking the stillness,
and making the future uncertain.

I see you now and I wonder;
what will you make of this third act?

Will you seek the Lord,
and let him heal you—

losing yourself,
and giving yourself in love?

Perhaps your next name,
who knows what that will be,

could it be one written on a white stone?

Enough

"I want to do what will make you proud of me," I say to her.

"Of course I'm proud of you" she says.

"I know. You have to say that" I say.

You are my mother.

I am proud.

I mean to do the things that you love and care about,
to let you know how I love you.

I do love you.

I love you.

You don't need to prove it.

To seal it then. And prove it to myself.

You just are, and you are enough.

But I am alone.

With nothing to prove, now what am I?

I don't know what you are, but—

you are enough.

Seeking

Sometimes I sit
thinking only of you—

My heart grows calm
as tears fall from my eyes.

Sometimes I walk
watching my steps—

but my mind and my heart
are only with you.

If only my arms
could find you to hold.

If only my eyes
could see you again.

All that I hear
is only clatter—
that which isn't
Your voice.

I shake my head
to clear the noise.

I call Your name,
and I call Your name.

I call Your name
in my lonely heart.
How long
must we be apart?

As I sit
tears are falling from my eyes—

for what I've been,
what I am,
and what I may become.

These tears
are of sorrow, and of joy—

for what was,
and is,
and is to come.

Her Name

Her name meant
stability,
solidity,
to me.

Like something granite;
Mt Rushmore.
Or something tectonic;
Australia.

Now I see her name;
and I remember she has gone—

my mind stops.

If minds could lose their breath,
mine would gasp,
and struggle to restart.

Conceive the inconceivable;
Australia sinking,
Mt Rushmore dissolving.

Has she truly left this earth?

Her name engraved in granite,
her soul amongst the stars?

Woman,
like grass and shadows,
is timed to wilt and fade,
by the measure of the sun.

Earth,
abiding still,
yet timed as well,
awaits a similar fate.

Granite melts in fervent heat.
Her name, eternal memory.

And both will be remade;
when Christ returns again.

A Time Apart

Fly away dear one.
Shed this world
and enter dreams
of tomorrow.

Lift your thoughts
upon the wind,
and let the sun's rays
carry them, and you
to unknown places.

There is a home,
made especially for you
in that celestial land.

We will gather,
and wonder.
Our thoughts also drifting,
here among the silent spaces
within ourselves.

As the clock's rhythmic
ticking calls us back
to remembrance
of our own beating hearts.

We look gratefully
into each other's eyes,
while remembering,
and appreciating,
all that you are to us.

III.

Two Roads Untaken

Two roads diverged in a yellow wood,
And sorry I could not travel either,
For having tripped upon my laces I no longer stood,
And upon my face there I brood,
And nevertheless enjoyed this unexpected breather.

The cool earthen soil was refreshing,
And though my plans had changed,
I looked upon those paths with no lamenting,
Nor for the steps I'd not be taking,
For I had rather found my peace there as I dreamed.

There stood a man before me all in white,
I thought that all my wits had come unglued,
He spoke such words as to delight,
He showed me what is wrong and what is right,
And laid my life before me to review.

When I awoke still at the crossing,
The sun was much lower in the sky,
With haste I tied my lacing,
And stood again to find the path that I'd be tracing,
A newer road with greater purpose before I die.

Footsteps in the Snow

Five men walking through the snow,
walking neither fast nor slow,
no man talking as they go,
five men walking in a row.

Dressed in black from head to toe,
like ravens black against the snow,
beneath their cloaks with heads bowed low,
fighting through the wind's cruel blow.

Ahead a tree of gnarled boughs,
an arching, twisting, silent gallows,
the sun's stark rays casts its shadows,
like Christ's arms stretched across their brows.

Each man arrives at his own tempo,
each casting off his earthly sorrow,
with hope enkindled for tomorrow,
these men together with face aglow.

Why do they travel through the snow,
and suffer through the wind's cruel blow,
to stand beneath this silent gallows,
and offer up their earthly sorrows?

To find true freedom from sin's law,
through Christ the healer of every flaw,
in praise of God with fear and awe,
to sing forever—

Allelujah!

The Signpost*

Just past midway
upon the journey
my soul slackened its pace,
to find a moment's rest,
and found a hidden place.

Beneath the trees,
among the grasses,
there stood a sign which read—

'Be well, and sortle in this place
but not to slumber relaxicated.
To those prone to urbumpkining
dethrope, unbeam and enpeacelate.'

Perhaps this trek had been too dear
my mind muddled from the strain.
The meaning of these words
was hidden from my brain.

I drew closer to the sign
to bring focus to my mind.
As the words they carried on—

'Despair not, insprevelent!
Philathea aleatin,
bemosphorel intayalen.
All life is made: a Sacrament!'

Alas I had a footing
to discern this cryptic writing.
Just enough of native tongue
encouraged me to carry on—

"These words writ for discovery,
present symbolic mystery,
what cannot be known mentally,
can be unearthed noetically."

Then I had a glimpsing
and a notion of its meaning,
a still and silent whispering
and a prayer within me stirring.

I mused as I continued on—

"Perhaps I'm not midway at all,
but have barely just begun."

*Glossary of new vocabulary in notes at back of book.

Pray First

Pray first,
and pray always—
every good thing
springs forth from the fertile soil
of prayer.

Prayer is the mother
of all virtues,
and the womb
of all noble thoughts.

In prayer,
we reach out to the Spirit,
and His Fruits
are placed in our hands.

There is no thievery
in prayer.
It is supplication,
and a gift of mercy—
freely given.

Prayer is a fertile field,
filled with wheat,
flowing in waves,
sun-drenched, and golden.

The very Bread
of Life
is risen in the ovens
of prayer.

Pray first,
and pray always.

A Dog's Prayer

Pride has me locked in a cage, where I sit;
indulging my selfish desires willingly,
and becoming bloated by them.

My eyes refuse to gaze beyond these confines;
while everything they see,
appears as a reflection only of me.

Free me from this squalor that I've loved;
don't let me be the dog
that returns to his vomit.

Let me be the little dog;
who gathers crumbs beneath Your table,
and feeds upon Your flesh.

Train my eyes to see only you, O Lord—
my ears to hear only your voice, O Master.

This pride has left me in the cold;
a heart, where dwells my vanity,
in sweet and sickly emptiness.

Please don't leave me here throughout this night;
but let me sleep upon Your bed,
and feel the warmth that is Your love.

Call me from this dog's house,
into the Master's chamber,
and let me gaze into Your eyes.

Place me on your leash and lead me—
tether me to Your mercy,
and don't let me stray.

I will wait at the door, until You return;
come to me, and let me be—

by your side forever.

Hidden Prayer, For Hidden Fruits

Everything
begins its life veiled,
beneath the surface,
and hidden from view.

Cultivate your inner soil
through prayer—
before the plant is seen,
roots are growing
below the surface.

The field that appears fallow,
or barren,
will bloom in time—
the persistent farmer
eventually harvests his reward.

Words are the clothing
our thoughts
and motives wear,
when visiting others.

But we disrobe entirely
in the presence of
The One who made us.

There are no clothes
to hide our thoughts
from Him.

Our forebearers
picked forbidden fruits,
but we, through prayer,
will bear the hidden fruits.

Love's Pure Light

There is something so simple and so sublime
in the beauty of love expressed, from one to another;
which we are gifted to witness,
which touches the heart,
and causes it to well up with abundant gratitude;
both for the one who has given their love,
and also for the one who has received it.

We love them both all the more for it.

There is a love too difficult to bear.
Is there?
I am thinking of a love that pierces our hearts;
that can cause our souls to bleed, if they could.

This is a love that overwhelms our senses,
which can scarcely be contained,
as if the fabric of our being is starting to tear, and to come apart;
for which all the tears ever cried will burst forth in a flood of joy
and pain—
as if we are giving birth to life, to an idea, to a new world within us;

and for each other.

Is there a love that can reveal the depths and the heights of life to
us simultaneously?
Is it possible to plumb down into the heart of the earth,
while also soaring through the clouds?

We have light, and sound, form and movement,
given freely to us from the hand of God,
all of which fill us with this kind of love—
an excruciating magnanimity.

This life, so solid and bright,
it fills us with laughter and beauty;

a light, reflecting from the shapes of our loves.
In this, we move about and have our being.

This life, so paper thin and fragile;
a tear in the paper can take these forms away,
as they fall into the shifting shadows, and disappear.

How can this life be so wide, so expansive, and stretch us so far?
It is an exquisite radiance with a numbing darkness intertwined.

How I wish that it were pure light.

The Crystal Doorway

This, for those afraid of the grave—
and who among us isn't?

(moldy, wet and dark with images of worms,
and creepy things)

But what of light, and breezes:
imagine the grave, up in the air—

a crystal-lined prism cut into the sky;
rectangular and brimming with brightness.

Up into this portal we are raised,
from which our souls emerge,
resplendent, on the other side.

Passing through this open door
we enter into the vastness
of our new home.

Perhaps this is so—
as we are lowered into the earth,
we are also lifted up,
through the crystal doorway.

Grave and doorway—
mirror images,
reflected about this life
on Earth.

IV.

The Poplars

Three poplars rising to the sky
reaching upward impossibly high
towering over this earth and me
they tell a tale of eternity.

Like Jacob's ladders side by side
these poplars joining earth to sky
or if they're seen the other way 'round
like heavenly arms reaching to the ground.

Their crenelated tops swaying in the breeze
sunlight dances upon their leaves
each leaf an angel, each branch a rung
ascending, descending angels in the sun.

Swelling, contracting their branches are spun
inhaling, exhaling like an enormous lung
their breathing speaks of hidden lives
beneath, behind this veiled world of mine.

Beneath the earth their roots entwined
all three sharing one life we find
appearing as distinct entities
these poplars instead, are just one tree.

A symbol of the Trinity
God made for us this poplar tree
the form and symbol very clear
yet subtler made in sun and air.

Around and through these trees the rays
of sun and wind about them plays
the Son, the Spirit and the Father
on full display through states of matter.

Cleaning House

Like longtime friends,
these habitual sins,
again and again,
make their home within.

Closer than family,
they know us innately,
fond of their company,
we invite them to stay.

We know that we shouldn't,
we said that we wouldn't,
we may act like we couldn't,
yet we've made them co-tenants.

They people our thoughts,
doing away with all oughts,
we gave, and they got
to scheme and to plot.

How long will they stay?
At least they should pay,
here day after day,
but what can I say?

We're housemates you know,
'round the fires warm glow,
these sins and I show,
that we're friends here below.

All greasy and comfortable,
neck deep in our meals,
gluttons 'round the table,
we like how we feel.

In the basement with despair,
sucking out all the air,
while I play solitaire,
through dirty windows we stare.

In the pool, on the patios,
my lusts dance and carouse.
Images from daydreams,
let out giggles and screams.

Feeling popular and famous,
these crowds intravenous,
with raised glasses they cheer me,
in my mind it's a party.

Overhead and around me,
pride's my structural framing.
With self-love as my floor,
vanity's my front door.

Mine is a tower on a hill,
flashy and glittery-gilt.
Specters of fame and of stars,
fill this house made of cards.

My guests are all clamorous,
freeloaders and odorous.
They are having a ball,
while I trip and I fall.

And of vice these are many,
each one costing me plenty.
Though their promises generous,
my debt's growing more onerous.

I'll kick them to the curb,
where they'll no longer perturb.
But oh how entirely absurd,
that I find I'm immured.

The need here is great,
I should not hesitate.
My house is unsound,
but I find myself bound.

Looking for an ally,
to crash this mad party,
a Spiritual Strongman
to put this intrusion to an end.

He'll send them off packing,
with a thorough tongue-lashing,
give my house a clean sweep,
then I'll have a sound sleep.

Once my house is set right,
from its devilish plight,
and my mind is set free,
from this demonic jamboree;

I'll give my house a remodel,
with thoughts godly and noble,
and through self-discipline and prayer,
this fixer-upper I'll repair.

A Call to Arms

Lord God disturb the peace
that my complacency enjoys.

Bring war and unrest
to my world-weariness.

Mercilessly stab the heart
of my selfish complaints.

Bring death to the nest
where anger sleeps within me.

Cut off the head of my pride
and cast me to my knees.

Do all of this I pray,

that I may find freedom,

and see clearly—

Your Kingdom.

An Audience with The King

Incense coils upward,
in long argentine strands,
angelic voices sing a joyous refrain—

"Receive the body of Christ,
taste the Fountain of Immortality."

The hands of Christ serve
the body of Christ,
from a golden chalice.

Each member called by name—
singular, and unique.

Forming a line in quiet expectation
of the gift of eternal blessings—

a body numerous are
the servants of The King—
multiform,
and manifesting,
His infinite creativity.

Let us each put on
the eyes of thanksgiving,
and the ears of obedience,
and praise.

Laying aside all earthly cares,
let us settle into that peace
which reveals things
as they truly are—

without judgement,
or condemnation,

but in the simplicity
of Godly revelation.

The Body and the Blood—
we receive,
and Christ receives us.

We are glorified by His glory,
and deified by His divinity.

We come to the King empty-handed,
and He gives us everything.

Keith (A Man of Silent Sacrifice)

At just nineteen he took possession of a mighty B-17,
   The Army Air Corp's durable workhorse
   Continental Europe's liberating air force
   The bomber known as The Flying Fortress,
He signed his name on the dotted line, to pilot this war-machine.

No longer a boy in forty-three, he took to the skies in battle,
   On December 5 to Paris and back
   Then Kiel, Ludwigshafen and Osnabruck
   Ringing in the New Year over Cognac,
Five missions into a long campaign, he's a man not easily rattled.

     A man of silent sacrifice
     Of the special ones who fly
     Young men who defend us
     War eagles of the sky.

A modest spiral notebook logs the record of his tour,
   In columns, names and dates and years
   No embellishments or fanfare
   Thirty missions in European air,
A marathon of horror that most men could not endure.

The logbook doesn't tell the tale of the courage, fear and loss,
   Friends like brothers gone too soon
   Flak and Messerschmitts at noon
   In dense fog the barrage balloons,
Nor does it mention his receiving the Distinguished Flying Cross.

     A man of silent sacrifice
     Of the special ones who fly
     Humble warriors who protect us
     Liberators of the skies.

His was the lead position, throughout life as in the war,
  Husband, father, grandpapa
  Honor, duty, fidelity
  Service was his earthly call,
Giving all on every mission, and leaving nothing more.

Upon his final flight from earth, the stars bright in the sky,
  The moon casting the fields aglow
  Cultivated row upon row
  Stars above and stripes below,
Our nation's banner, as God's creation, enfolds him in its glory.

    A man of silent sacrifice
    Of the special ones who die
    Our fathers who watch over us
    The sentinels of the sky.

The Well-Dressed Man

Today I saw a well-dressed man,
in all the proper brands.

His backpack made by Arcteryx,
shirt and coat made of Spandex.

A water bottle in one hand,
a coffee mug the other.

His feet adorned by Adidas,
his eyes with RayBan sunglasses.

His hair was clipped and cropped just right,
his skin the proper hue.

His pants were neither loose nor tight—
all done, no more to do.

A modern symbol of perfection,
with just a hint of intimidation:

an image of success,
designing to impress.

Awed I was it must be admitted,
but also very irritated.

The effort I admired,
but it also made me tired.

While in my angst he took a call,
and clearly it was trouble.

His entire demeanor took a fall,
he's simply not a god at all.

In his disgrace I felt my shame,
my judgement and my blame.

This man who so well dresses,
betrayed my prejudices.

Repenting of my first condemning,
vowing for a life amending.

No matter whether prince or pauper,
All men deserve my love and honor.

Stair Dweller

I saw a man on a stairwell today,
sitting on the floor.

I passed him quickly on my way,
a glance and nothing more.

His image though now haunts me,
a working man not free.

A man like me, living on these stairs,
diligent yet in despair.

This is the world we've made for him,
homes and bread for profit.

Where prices rise and futures dim,
life lived out of pocket.

He smiled at me and cracked a joke,
his spirit still unbroke.

I realized then though life is tough,
strong wills can be enough.

And while the world can seem unfair,
if each can just forbear—

we'll find some peace and joy just like,

the dweller on the stair.

Good Medicine

I watched the news today,
and heard the world spinning round.

I did my work today,
and put my shoulder to the ground.

I earned and spent and
kept the world going round.

But in my mind,
as work ground me into the ground—

my thoughts kept spinning,
round and round:

leaving me with little sense
of what's up, and what is down.

Like a botox injection
to the inner man—

our worldly lives,
lived out through worldly plans.

Hearts paralyzed by fear and debt,
with no recourse but to worry and to fret.

There is an antidote to
worldliness however—
an inoculation given
by Christ, our deliverer.

Nursing us back
to wholeness,
with the medicine
of blessedness.

By faith and hope
within our hearts,

we forge a union
that love imparts.

Our thoughts may swirl
like an epic tornado,

but a peace will rise up
as a conquering hero.

We think we are alone
in this world,

yet in our hearts
we will find that pearl—

the one for which we
sell all we possess,

to live in peaceful holiness.

V.

A Short, Short History of A Thought

A thought crept up out of the dark
and whispered into my ear—

but then vanished into the fog
from which all new thoughts emerge,

before I could catch it,

turn it over,

and examine its underbelly.

An Addendum to the Aforementioned Short History

I dropped a line into the abyss,
where thoughts dwell—

after a time I felt a tug,
and pulling hard:

I yanked an embryonic idea,
half-baked,
and somewhat unformed,
from the gray-matter sediment.

I mulled it for a time,
and placed it in a jar.

The rest I stuffed into my pocket,

to chew on later.

War

I witnessed two altercations;
a theme with variations.

Men fighting over a patch of pavement;
Dogs fighting over a piece of excrement.

The stakes seemed about equal;
The contestants pitched in battle.

With fury they attacked;
Each on the others back.

Autos jockeying for the pole position;
Canines chewing on an old emission.

Skirmishes with a tragicomic ending;
Car crashes and a lot of foul digesting.

As I mentioned I saw two battles;
and the stakes were nearly equal.

The Spider and The Fly

Am I the spider,
or am I the fly?

Busily making my webs,
or being trapped by them?

Layer upon layer of silky threads,
wrapping, encasing, and hardening.

Ambitious and industrious,
dizzy and nauseous.

Round, round and round,
spinning, spinning and spinning.

Am I the spinner,

or am I the spun?

A Power of Persuasion

"Don't give them treats,
don't give them treats,
don't give them treats."

I repeat to myself over,
and over,
and over again.

As a mantra against the power
of their big brown eyes,
as they look up into mine—
and attempt to hypnotize me.

"Give us treats,
give us treats,
give us treats."

They say in diverse,
unspoken,
yet persuasive ways.

My mind tells me,
"they don't need treats,
it will make them fat."

And this makes excellent sense.
Even so,
I feel my resolve weakening,
as their gaze works its
magic.

Little round faces,
like little moons
with button noses.

Fur lined penumbras
and pouty lips (if dogs have lips).

Their little tails wagging
in unison,
like fluffy windshield wipers—

Back and forth,
back and forth,
back and forth.

I watch these for a moment,
and feel myself dropping
into a trance,
And I begin to say:

"Give them treats,
give them treats,
give them treats."

And I concur.

Yes, an excellent idea.

The Shepherd of Swallows

They swirl and they spin,
darting this way and that.

They are hard to follow,
and hard to catch.

Like swallows,
they are lively,
and ever-moving,
and rarely seem to sleep;

and even in our sleep,
they keep moving.

Our thoughts,
are never still,

our minds
in motion—

perpetual.

We need a shepherd,
and a guide.

With words,
like trained falcons,
the prayers of the church,
disrupt our swallow's
erratic motions—

and flying in formation,
they bring our thoughts—

into line.

How do you catch a swallow,
and put it in a cage?

Very difficult...

But fly alongside—
as they swirl,
be their guide.

With prayers,
they will follow
by your side—

and find safe

landing.

Tears & Freedom

What tears have you shed;
that I've not shed also?

What tears could I cry;
that you couldn't cry too?

What fear is there then, in sharing our pain—
one with another?

What loss could there be, in healing this shame—
between us?

***

Through this vale of tears,
behind veils, to hide our tears;
each walk, inside their fears,
yearning to break free.

Fear and shame divide us,
as dismal cloaks they hide us—
obscuring the depths behind our eyes,
and recognition of our common lives.

Tears are not a driving rain;
for driving us apart.
Tears are a revealing rain;
exposing each one's heart.

And tears can be a healing rain—
enabling us to grow.

***

What sorrows have we known;
that Christ has not first known?

What suffering will we face;
that He has not embraced?

Upon our cross, all falsehood falls aside;
the fabric of our lives is torn asunder,
revealing a wedding garment under,
and truth proclaims we are Christ's bride—

Jesus claims His bride,
looks long into our eyes,
lifts our veil of tears,

and from our shame and fears—

Christ frees us.

The Time of Our Lives

What a beautiful day!

It's sunny, it's rainy,
it's cold or it's hot,
it's what we had wanted,
or else it is not—

It doesn't get any better than this,
we are having the time of our lives.

In all things be joyful,
in all things be thankful,
in all things praise our God—

for making us,
and setting us,
in this place and time.

This is the time of our lives.

We're sad and we're happy,
we've lost and found gain,
we're old and we're young,
in health and in pain—

This is the time of our lives.

From everlasting to everlasting,
from beginning to end;
Was, and Is, and Is To Come—
and nothing new, here under the sun.

They had their fun,
and they'll have it too,
just as we do—
We'll all have this time for our lives.

Don't wait for tomorrow—
do it today!

The Kingdom at hand—
seize the day!

The time in our lives,
when Christ arrives—

Now it will be,

The time of our lives!

NOTES

I.

MANY TEARS—

Upon the death of my mother, and for a time subsequent to this, I was lost and in a fog. I couldn't will the 'fog' away and found little relief. Psalm 30:5 reminded me 'that weeping may endure for a night, but joy comes in the morning'.

This truth eluded me, until eventually I confronted my sorrows and the depth of my loss, particularly through a preponderance of tears, and by way of this, the 'fog' finally lifted and I could see the potential for a bright and hopeful future again.

In the Orthodox Christian tradition we sing a song entitled, "Many Years", as a celebration of birthdays, anniversaries and patron saint name days. The title for this poem is a play on that one, and is a celebration of tears as a means of processing grief and of healing.

TRUE HOME—

In My Father's house are many mansions; if it were not so, I would have told you. I go to prepare a place for you. (John 14:2)

THE TREMOR—

Mickey Spillane was a famous crime novelist in the 1950s onward. From my experience, he is the most well-known and recognized of the Spillanes. His novels were tough and gritty and displayed the cultural icons and archetypes as described in this poem.

NOT A RHETORICAL PROBLEM—

This title came to mind, because the problem of death and loss is not a theoretical or rhetorical one, nor is it a poetic device to elicit insights. It is very real, and demands real solutions and answers.

However, so much about this problem is shrouded in mystery, but one thing is certain, in my opinion; that God's love and the power of love instilled in each one of us is the spark that can rekindle our lives and renew purpose and meaning in our lives.

SHEDDING—

For you yourselves know perfectly that the day of the Lord so comes as a thief in the night. (1 Thessalonians 5:2)

..."If you abide in My word, you are my disciples indeed. And you shall know the truth, and the truth shall make you free." (John 8:31-32)

All the lies we tell ourselves, the fantasies we live by, the untruths we express, will be taken from us when we abide in, and with Jesus Christ. The loss of these illusions and fantasies, like death, is painful, but in the end, the truth in Christ is ennobling and deifying.

THE ASTOUNDING WORDS OF JOB—

"Naked I came from my mother's womb, and naked shall I return there. The Lord gave and the Lord has taken away; Blessed be the name of the Lord." (Job 1:21)

Elisabeth Kubler-Ross, *On Death and Dying* (1969) In this book the author describes, among other things, the five typical stages of grief in dealing with death.

II.

IMPRINTING—

God gave me a loving mother. He surrounds us all with love and mercy. The things of this world that we love and that love us, are all wonderful but temporal. The birthplace of all these things and the source of all love is only in God. In stillness, and in our heart, we can cultivate this primary and essential relationship with the source of all love.

WAITING—

God allows our hearts to be broken to cause us to sincerely seek him, and to bring us back into relationship with Him. Our hunger is not for food, or for what we can get from those we love, or from the things of this world, but ultimately our hunger is only for God Himself.

THREE NAMES—

...as many of us as were baptized into Christ Jesus, were baptized into his death....Now if we have died with Christ, we believe that we shall also live with Him...(Romans 6:3,8)

Hesychasm: The practice of stillness in the presence of God.

"And I will give him a white stone, and on the stone a new name written which no one knows except him who receives it." (Revelation 2:17)

SEEKING—

A poem about my mom but also about God; actually more about God.

HER NAME—

One generation passes away, and another generation comes; but the earth abides forever. (Ecclesiastes 1:4)

...and the elements will melt with fervent heat; both the earth and the works that are in it will be burned up. (2 Peter 3:10)

Now I saw a new heaven and a new earth, for the first heaven and the first earth had passed away. (Revelation 21:1)

III.

TWO ROADS UNTAKEN—

This poem is inspired and is a response to Robert Frost's famous poem, "The Road Not Taken". In my poem, God asserts a third way, one apart from the options we make for ourselves, and one with greater potential for fulfillment and less potential for self-delusion.

FOOTSTEPS IN THE SNOW—

The concept for this poem originated in a poignant dream I had in my youth about five men, monks, traveling through the snow, through the trials of this life, on their way to union with God; giving up their lives here, and suffering through hardships now for Christ, in order to gain eternal life.

"If anyone desires to come after Me, let him deny himself, and take up his cross, and follow Me. For whoever desires to save his life will lose it, but whoever loses his life for My sake will find it." (Matthew 16:24-25)

THE SIGNPOST—

The mysteries of life and faith seem to be revealed over time as we mature in faith. This poem is about discovery of God as we travel the path leading to Him: some things are known, some known only partially, some are revealed by experience, some are yet to be discovered, and some things may never be understood.

Glossary:

Sortle: a gentle rest for the soul; but one that includes a watchfulness and readiness for spiritual battle.

Relaxicated: taking rest to an unhealthy extreme, leading to a sort of intoxication, sloth or laziness.

Urbumpkining: derision or prejudice aimed at others, acting in an arrogantly derisive way.

Dethrope: an act of humble abdication; to dethrone one's pride while simultaneously disrobing one's self-esteem and vanity.

Unbeam: to focus on one's own vices for the purpose of becoming virtuous; to 'remove the beam from one's own eye and not to focus on the speck in another's eye'.

Enpeacelate: to actively and intentionally seek a state of inner stillness; to set aside that which creates discord.

Insprevelent: to find inspiration in the created world and see God's revelation through the everyday things of life; sometimes used as an expression, or exclamation of encouragement.

Noetically: done through the nous or the intellect, but not reason; instead from the heart or from the depths of the soul.

A DOG'S PRAYER—

As a dog returns to his own vomit, so a fool repeats his folly. (Proverbs 26:11)

And she said, "Yes Lord, yet even the little dogs eat the crumbs which fall from their master's table." Then Jesus answered and said to her, "O woman, great is your faith! Let it be as you desire." (Matthew 15:27-28)

"I am the living bread which came down from heaven. If anyone eats of this bread, he will live forever; and the bread that I shall give is My flesh, which I shall give for the life of the world." (John 6:51)

IV.

THE POPLARS—

Then he dreamed, and behold, a ladder was set up on the earth, and its top reached to heaven; and there the angels of God were ascending and descending on it. (Genesis 28:12)

CLEANING HOUSE—

No one can enter a strong man's house and plunder his goods unless he first binds the strong man. And then he will plunder his house. (Mark 3:27)

But when a stronger than he comes upon him and overcomes him, he takes from him all his armor in which he trusted, and divides the spoils. (Luke 11:22)

In this case Christ is the stronger man who will come and plunder what was taken originally by the sins that overcame and bound us.

When an unclean spirit goes out of a man, he goes through dry places, seeking rest, and finds none. Then he says, 'I will return to my house from which I came.' And when he comes, he finds it empty, swept, and put in order. Then he goes and takes with him seven other spirits more wicked than himself, and they enter and dwell there; and the last state of that man is worse than the first. (Matthew 12:43-45)

Through an alliance with the stronger man, Christ, we can fill our houses, after they are swept clean, so there is no room for the unclean spirits to return. Christ gives us the grace and power to carry this out if we are also willing to work with Him, and follow His commands.

AN AUDIENCE WITH THE KING—

In the Divine Liturgy of the Orthodox Church this hymn is sung, "Receive the body of Christ, taste the Fountain of Immortality..." as the body of Christ, the members of the church, come forward to receive the body and blood of Christ in the Eucharist.

Like a receiving line, each of us gets our chance, and our time to be received by The King of All, Christ our Lord; and each of us, unique elements of the body of Christ, are transformed little by little into the image and likeness of Christ as we receive and eat of His flesh and His blood every week.

As we are made anew in Christ, we find that we can more easily lay aside our earthly cares, and set aside our old ways of thinking: judging and condemning, and in their place we can fill our senses and our spirits with thanksgiving, praise and purity.

KEITH (A MAN OF SILENT SACRIFICE)—

A tribute poem to my step-father who rarely spoke of his time flying in WWII but through a simple little mission logbook we found in a box in his closet, along with his commendations and medals, we learned a lot about his sacrifice and service.

GOOD MEDICINE—

The kingdom of heaven is like a merchant seeking beautiful pearls, who, when he had found one pearl of great price, went and sold all that he had and bought it. (Matthew 13:45)

TEARS & FREEDOM—

The vale of tears, or valley of tears, is a term describing the sorrows and sufferings of this life, in this world.

None of us enjoys suffering or sorrow yet, in accepting these and willingly taking up our own cross, and following Jesus our Lord, through these difficulties God refines us, our falsehoods fall away, and we are made anew and given new life in Christ. From this, the life we lived before is torn away, and we lose it, revealing our true life. (Luke 17:33 and Matthew 16:25)

We are called to a true life, as members of Christ's church, as members of His body—as His bride. As such, He loves us and cares for us and frees us from our enslavement to sin, shame and corruption.

THE TIME OF OUR LIVES—

Rejoice always, pray without ceasing, in everything give thanks; for this is the will of God for you in Christ Jesus. (1 Thessalonians 5:16-18)

Chronos Time: chronological or sequential time; the time of clocks: of days, weeks and years; the measure of our lives in time.

Kairos Time: the appropriate and opportune time for an action or event; the time that God acts, and the time we can act in synergy with God.

"I am the Alpha and the Omega, the Beginning and the End," says the Lord, "who is and who was and who is to come, the Almighty." (Revelations 1:8)

That which has been is what will be, that which is done is what will be done, and there is nothing new under the sun. (Ecclesiastes 1:9)

People past, present and future all have this opportunity of life, and of seeking God if they choose.

We live in the juxtaposition of Chronos and Kairos time; our lives are measured by Chronos time, but our actions towards or away from God have eternal consequences; God acts in our lives through Kairos time, while our response also has a Kairos meaning and purpose.

ABOUT THE AUTHOR

Francis Spillane lives in the state of Washington with his wife Patty and their two dogs, Fritz and Rocco. New poems, as well as daily inspirational quotes from the early fathers of the Christian faith can be found on his blogsite: prayerfullife.blog

68036015R00063

Made in the USA
Lexington, KY
29 September 2017